Coin Magic

by the editors of Klutz

KLUTZ®

KLUTZ®

is an independent publishing company staffed entirely by real human beings. We began our corporate life back in 1977 in a Palo Alto, California garage that we shared with a Chevrolet Impala. Back then, founders John Cassidy, Darrell Lorentzen and B.C. Rimbeaux were all students and one of the founding principles was thusly stated: Be in and out of business by the end of summer vacation.

So much for that plan.

Plan B? Create the best-written, best-looking, most imaginative books in the world. Be honest and fair in all our dealings. Work hard to make every day feel like the first day of summer vacation.

We aim high.

We'd love to hear your comments about this book. **Write us.**

KLUTZ®

455 Portage Avenue
Palo Alto, CA 94306

www.klutz.com

Book and latex square
manufactured in Malaysia, coin in U.S.A. ✱

Additional Copies:
Give us a call at (650) 857-0888 and we'll help track down your nearest Klutz retailer. Should they be out of stock, additional copies of this book as well as the entire library of 100% Klutz certified books are available in the Klutz Catalog. See the last page for details.

✱Coin intended for magic tricks only. Don't spend it.

Stop!
Read this Page!

The Magician's Oath

Before you go any further, you have to take the Oath.

If you can't take it, or keep it, you'll never be an Amazing Magician surrounded with mystery, you'll only be the forgettable owner of a few cheesy tricks that everyone knows (because you showed them how). Not only that, but Houdini's ghost will haunt you for seven years. Here's the Oath. Please stand up.

Place your hand upon this book and repeat the following:

I (YOUR NAME HERE) do solemnly swear **never** to reveal how any of my tricks are done. Nor will I ever do any trick twice in a row for the same audience. No matter how much they **hound** me or even beat me to a pulp. I will be **true** to my secrets. I understand that if I break this oath, this book will burst into flames, my hair will turn to pasta and my teeth **will rot in a day.** Thank you very much.

How to Palm a **Coin** Three Ways

The first lesson in Magic 101 is learning how to palm a coin, how to keep it in a hand without anyone suspecting it's there. Magicians use at least nine basic coin palms, and each has variations. Here, we'll just show you three: **The Finger Palm** (our favorite); the **Two Finger Clip** (nice, easy, handy); and the **Classic** (very tough, but no book on coin magic would be complete without it).

The Finger Palm

If you're only going to learn one palm out of this book, make it this one. It's the simplest, and for most of your purposes, it's all you'll ever need. Start by examining a hand hanging naturally by your side—fingers bent, slightly open. Then bring it up for a closer look and turn it over, palm up. Slide a quarter (or nickel if it fits better) into the spot shown on the illustration.

Innocent

Guilty

Then, coin in place, drop your hand back down to your side. Does it look identical?

If it doesn't, keep practicing... practicing... practicing...

5

Two Finger Clip

A small but handy little palm. Not quite as easy as the basic Finger Palm, but you'll need it for a proper Shuttle Pass, which you'll be learning here in a second. The coin is held (clipped) between the two fingers as shown. When it's done correctly, the back of your hand looks loose and entirely natural. You can practice the Two Finger Clip by working on a **Shuttle Pass.**

The **Shuttle Pass** is quite direct. You show off a nickel, then drop it into the other hand where it turns into a quarter instantaneously.

Your View

- ▶

1 Finger Palm a quarter and keep that hand turned down. In the other hand, show off your nickel.

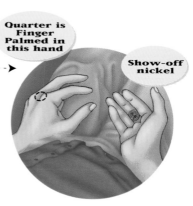

Quarter is Finger Palmed in this hand

Show-off nickel

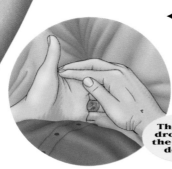

2 Then simply fake-drop it to your other hand as shown. Keep the nickel in place by using the Two Finger Clip.

The fake drop. Get the timing down.

3 Then, instantly, reveal the quarter. The key to the move is timing. The two hands come together smoothly, naturally. Do it right, and your audience will swear you dropped a coin from one hand to the other.

As in a lot of coin magic, the way to practice is to study reality in a mirror. Take a coin and REALLY drop it from one hand to the other. Then fake it. Then really do it. Then fake it. When the two look identical, you're there.

Audience View

The fake drop

Palm

We're including this one because everyone wants to learn it. **At first.** But the Classic is very tough to do properly. No one learns to do it well in less than two weeks of frustrating effort. BUT, if you're a committed kind of tricky person, it's the most versatile palm of them all. They don't call it the Classic for nothing. Every decent coin magician in the world uses it.

Let your hands hang at your sides for a moment. Now, without moving them, look down at one of them. Are the fingers stiff and straight and weird-looking? **(Answer: No.)** Does the hand look flat and tense? **(Answer: No.)** Does it look bent, relaxed, natural? **(Answer: Yes.)**

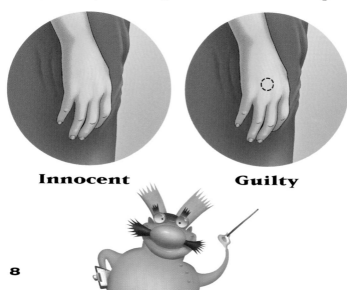

Innocent   **Guilty**

Now bring it up in the same naturally bent position and turn it over, palm up. What you're going to be practicing is a method of wedging a coin into the cup of your bent palm in such a way that the back of your hand looks no different than it does **right now**.

This is impossible. At least it seems that way. Use a quarter (a good palmable size for most kids) and stick it where the illustration shows. When you turn your palm over, the coin will fall out unless you stiffen your hand and put all the fingers in a weird position. You won't believe that anyone ever does this in a believable way.

When you first try it, it looks like this...

By the third day, though, you will start to have hope. Little coin-gripping muscles **will start developing**. By the end of two weeks you might even have it: a good-looking Classic Palm. You'll know when you have it by a simple test: Does your empty hand hanging by your side look **exactly** identical to your other hand, the one guiltily holding a coin in the Classic Palm? If both hands are identical, you pass.

...Two weeks later, it looks like this.

The Vanishing
Pants

Here's a trick for those unreasonable readers out there who want the impossible—killer magic with no practice. As always, the **story** is the magic, not the trick. Announce to your audience that, due to relentless popular demand, you are going to make your pants disappear "right before your very eyes!" Women will faint. Children will **scream.**

1 Put a quarter on your pant leg exactly as illustrated, about thigh high.

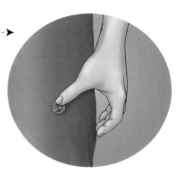

2 Catch a fold of fabric from underneath the quarter and keep your thumb on the coin while you fold the fabric over the quarter.

Trick continues on the next page.

11

3 The Key Move: I lied.

Actually, don't cover the quarter. LOOK like you're covering it. Instead, use your thumb to pull the coin up into your hand.

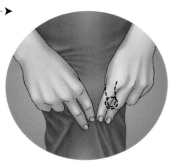

Thumb holds coin here.

4 Now just rub your fingers as shown over the place on your pants where the audience thinks the coin still is.

Talk about how good it feels to rub a coin through the fabric of your pants, through your skin, and into your leg, "where it can dissolve into my blood stream, instantly increasing the resale value of my body by 25 cents..."

5 Slowly unfold the flap to reveal the fact that, yes indeed, the coin has vanished and is even now coursing its way through your blood.

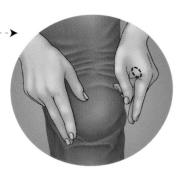

When your audience wants to look at your hands (and audiences always do) just use the guilty hand to cover your nose. One indelicate snort and drop the coin into your other hand waiting below. A bit disgusting, yes, but sometimes you have to stoop to these things.

P.S. Your audience wants to know about the disappearing pants? A misunderstanding. You meant to say the **coin** would disappear—**not** the pants!

Heavens!

T o x i c
Boxers and the
Vanishing Coin

As straight magic, this is a small little bit; but the accompanying story turns it into a **truly breathtaking production.**

What It Looks Like

You're holding a coin up high for all the world to see. You announce the fact that you are holding a coin and one pair of Dad's boxer shorts (actually, you can use anyone's boxer shorts).Then you begin to describe the following little-known scientific fact:

"People don't realize it, but scientists have been using coins to detect the presence of 'apparel gases' for many years.

Apparel gases are created when articles of personal clothing are subjected to extraordinary conditions and yet are not washed with enough frequency..."

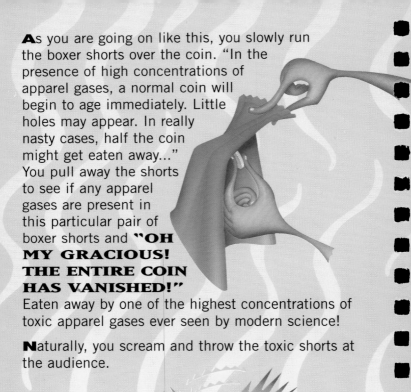

As you are going on like this, you slowly run the boxer shorts over the coin. "In the presence of high concentrations of apparel gases, a normal coin will begin to age immediately. Little holes may appear. In really nasty cases, half the coin might get eaten away..." You pull away the shorts to see if any apparel gases are present in this particular pair of boxer shorts and **"OH MY GRACIOUS! THE ENTIRE COIN HAS VANISHED!"** Eaten away by one of the highest concentrations of toxic apparel gases ever seen by modern science!

Naturally, you scream and throw the toxic shorts at the audience.

How to Do It

This is embarrassing. Hold the coin up high, directly in front of your shirt pocket. As you run the boxers over the coin, pick it up with the moving hand and drop it (the coin, not the boxers) into your pocket.

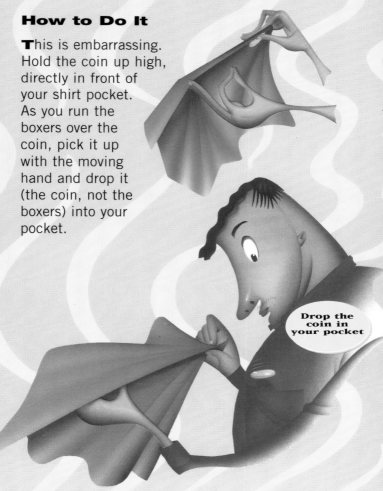

Drop the coin in your pocket

The boxers will keep the whole move invisible. **Rip** away the boxers and...**reveal both hands to be empty!**

That's it. Like I said, embarrassingly easy. Just make sure you play the story to the hilt.

17

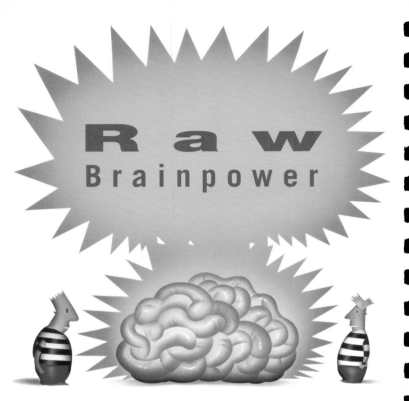

R a w
B r a i n p o w e r

You know you've got an incredible brain—no matter what your teachers think. The problem is, how do you make sure everyone else knows? Here, at last, is your foolproof system.

How It Goes

Get someone to toss a handful of change on the table. You count the heads. Flip one if you have to, but make sure the **number of heads** is even. Turn your back and issue the following commands to the audience.

Issuing The Five Commandments

1 "Turn over a coin."

2 "Turn over another coin."

3 "Turn over a pair of coins. Pick any two you want."

4 "Keep turning over pairs of coins. Do them two at a time, any two you like. It can even be coins you've already turned. Do this as long as you like. Quit whenever."

5 (After they've quit issue a last command): "Cover one coin with your hand." Then, turn around and say...

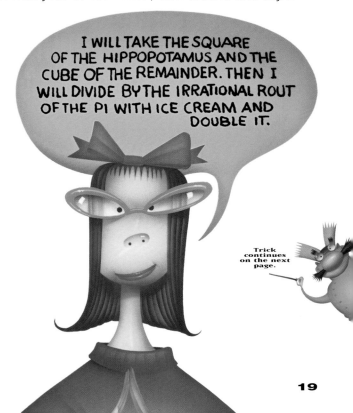

I WILL TAKE THE SQUARE OF THE HIPPOPOTAMUS AND THE CUBE OF THE REMAINDER. THEN I WILL DIVIDE BY THE IRRATIONAL ROUT OF THE PI WITH ICE CREAM AND DOUBLE IT.

Trick continues on the next page.

Then, announce what the covered coin is: heads or tails. You'll be right, and you'll be right for the next hundred times in a row if they think it was **all luck.**

How To Do It

When the handful is on the table, count just the heads and make sure the number is even. If it isn't, just flip a coin over and lie. Explain that you're checking to see if it's a real heads-or-tails coin.

So. The head count is even. You're positive. Turn around and ask a volunteer to go through all the instructions. When they finally quit, and they've covered a single coin with their hand, turn around and look mysterious. Start rattling off bogus equations. Meanwhile, check the head count again. If it's odd, the covered coin is heads. If it's even, it's tails. Works every time.

Remember it this way:

EVEN means the covered coin is tails.

ODD means heads.

Coin Snatching

This is a classic "uncle" trick. (Why? Because everybody's got an uncle who can do it.)

The idea is to set a coin on your arm, and then snatch it mid-air in one swell foop.

The first time you try this, incidentally, the coin will go rocketing off somewhere and be lost forever, so practice with pennies.

1 Arrange your arm as shown. Elbow very high, hand up by your ear. Set a coin as shown.

2 Then, mousetrap quick, bring your hand down and snatch the coin out of the air.

Now, as time goes on and you seek **greater** challenges, put **two** coins on your arm. Then, **three**. Then, **four**. I have heard of, but never seen, people who can do as many as **six**.

The Retention
Pass

This is another Basic Coin Magic Move you've got to learn. It takes some practice, but if it didn't, it wouldn't be so nice. It's used by professionals and you'll appreciate their skill all the more once you've learned it yourself.

How It Looks

A coin is held up for all to see and placed carefully on the palm of one hand. The fingers close convincingly around it, the audience sees the coin in place, and then the fingers open slowly to reveal— **nothing**. It's gone. Right in front of their eyes. Magicians call it the Retention Pass because the audience "retains" a view of the coin even when it's not there. **Totally baffling.**

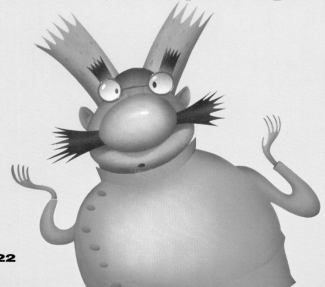

1 Extend a hand to one side, palm open.

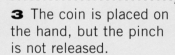

2 The other hand holds a coin in a pinch, revealing basically the entire thing. Use the thumb and middle finger.

3 The coin is placed on the hand, but the pinch is not released.

Trick continues on the next page.

4 One by one, the fingers close down over the coin.

5 They appear to be tight, but they're actually not.

6 The Dirty Work: Keep the coin. Pull it away as you move your guilty hand. Cover the dirty work with a pointing forefinger.

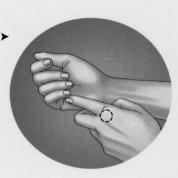

How To Do It?

The secret? Practice, practice, practice. Timing, timing, timing. I know from experience that grocery store check-out lines are an excellent place to work on this trick.

...The Low Point of This Book

Although we ourselves would **Never** stoop to potty humor, we'll include a small punchline to the Retention Pass here that uses a little of it for those of you who do not share our own high standards in these matters.

As you pretend to "hold" the coin in your empty fist, ask your audience if they've ever swallowed a coin. Tell them neither have you. ("But if I did, I bet it would hurt... ....twice.") Then put the empty fist to your mouth and suck noisily on it. Get big eyes and fake a big swallow. Then go through a little uncomfortable bit of fake digestion and reach behind you (with your hand that already has the coin) to pull it out. Hold your nose tightly and the coin at arm's length.

Fake the swallow

Say:

"EEE EEEEE WWW WWW WWW WWW WWW W"!!

The Unloseable Coin Toss

Everyone knows gambling is bad for you, so we've figured out a simple, effective way to take the risk out of your average coin toss. Learn this trick and coin tossing, for you at least, will no longer be a game of chance.

Pull out the coin, ask everyone to call it in the air, then give it a MAJOR heave into the air—a good twenty feet or so.

Holler **"Heads"** when it's up there (holler loud and first) and catch it. Then a quick slap onto the back of your hand and guess what? It's heads! And it'll be heads for the next 45 times in a row if you like.

Why? This is the embarrassing part...because you faked the whole toss.

You practiced the moves by yourself by really tossing the coin, so that part looks convincing. When the coin was "airborne", you tracked it with your eyes correctly; and when you "caught" the coin, you faked the right slap sound by snapping your fingers (practice, practice, practice).

Since the coin never leaves your hand, a quick glance before the "toss" is all you need to figure out if the slap on your hand is going to give you heads or tails.

In order to "sell" the whole thing, just toss naturally, move quickly, confidently, and get your timing down.

Pure wonderful fraud.

27

The

Trick
in This Book

We know who you are. You're a practice-hater. Instant gratification is your middle name.

But still. You have high standards. You want completely amazing, knock-'em-dead magic.

Fortunately, we're prepared for unreasonable people like you. We have an item right here that fits your immature needs quite nicely. It's called **The Amazing Sneezer Coin.**

aah

What It Looks Like

A coin sits on a table. You pick it up, toss it high into the air, where it vanishes at the peak of its arc. **("POOF! Where'd it go?")**

The audience looks at you, baffled. You shrug your shoulders, but at the same time you feel a sneeze starting to come on. **A big one.** Politely, you cover your nose and mouth and provide all the necessary disgusting sound effects during the huge build-up. When the explosion finally comes, wonder of wonders, what should drop into a volunteer's hand but the **missing coin!**

Slide the coin off the table

How to Do It

You're sitting at a table. The coin is sitting in front of you. Draw everyone's attention to the coin. Point at it. Talk about it. Make a HUGE deal out of that coin. Then pick it up by sliding the coin off the table. The easiest most natural way is to just slide it to the edge of the table and pick it up—all in the same sliding hand. So that's exactly what you do.

choo!

trick continues on the next page.

False. Actually, that's exactly what it looks like you did. You're a magician though. You don't really do anything the way it looks. You're sliding the coin all right, but you're sliding it entirely off the table and into your other hand which is waiting conveniently below.

But the audience doesn't know that. Everything looks normal. You hold up the empty hand exactly as if it had a quarter in it and say, **"Watch this quarter, folks."**

Then "toss" it high into the air. Follow it with your eyes to the peak...then...long pause...slowly look around. Where'd it go?

It vanished!

Big Tip: If you want a good looking fake, study the real thing first. How to do that? Simple. Really pick a coin off the table with the same sliding motion. (It's totally natural. You've done it a million times in your life already. You've just never really looked at it.) Examine the reality, and keep it in mind as you practice the fake. When the two look alike, you're there.

That's when everyone looks at you and you start to feel that **sneeze coming on**. Cover your mouth and nose with your guilty hand, the one that really does have the quarter, and at the explosive climax, grab someone by the wrist, put their hand under your nose, and drop the

quarter into it. Sniffle and little and say **"Thank you"**.

Then see if anyone wants to **examine your quarter more closely.**

Tornado
Coin Flip

Set a quarter on top of a table, right at the edge. Squat down and blow hard right over the top of the coin. It will flip and fly away.

For you budding scientists, I should explain that the quarter flips because you've lowered the air pressure right above it. The little vacuum you've created right over the quarter sucks it up just a fraction. When that happens, your breath catches it and flips it over.

Quarter + Nickel Half Gainer

Make a coin sandwich out of two quarters and a nickel and hold it exactly as shown—quarter/nickel/quarter. Drop the bottom quarter and nickel (but NOT the top quarter) into your other hand. **The drop should be one foot.**

Weird Fact: The quarter and nickel will always perform exactly one flip in mid-air and land in reverse order—quarter on top, nickel on bottom. Never fails.

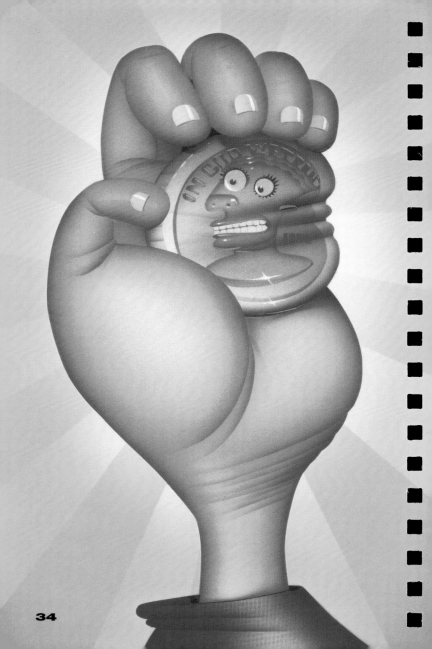

The Pulverized
Penny

What It Looks Like

You dig out a penny from your pocket and hold it up for all to see. You toss it back and forth from hand to hand for a second. Then, with it clenched in a fist, you announce the following:

"Using nothing but the awesome strength of my own bare hands, I am going to bend this coin before your very eyes!"

You get ready to begin squeezing the coin in your fist, but suddenly you stop. In order to soften up the molecular structure of the coin, you're going to need to bathe the coin in toxic fumes. So saying, open up your fist a little bit and ask a volunteer to breathe toxically into it. They do and then you begin squeezing with all your might. Just as the beads of sweat begin to appear on your brow, you open your hand and what should appear but the very penny—**bent!!**

Trick continues on the next page.

(How to get a bent penny? We recommend starting with a regular penny and using two pairs of pliers on it. Works every time.)

35

How to Do It

■It's time to learn the Bobo Switch, one of the most basic sleights in the world of coin magic. It's not an especially hard move—you'll be able to do it roughly within a minute or two. But making it appear absolutely perfect, that takes a little more time. Work on it in check-out lines and places like that.

- ->

1 Put a bent penny in the Finger Palm. This penny is a **secret** just between me and you. The audience knows nothing of it.

Bent penny is finger palmed in this hand.

◄- -

2 Pick up another penny. Toss it back and forth from hand to hand. (Don't let it clink against your secret bent coin.)

Toss the good penny back...

...and forth. Keep bent the penny hidden.

Good penny is finger palmed in this hand.

After a few tosses, pull the Bobo Switch. Hide the good coin and toss the bent one.

3 On the third toss, fake it. Toss the bent coin, and simultaneously slide the other one out of view in your fingers. This can be done so well that nobody without X-ray vision will spot the trickery.

The rest is all theatrics. Get a volunteer to breathe toxic fumes into your fist, then go on and on about your incredible strength. During all this, incidentally, all you need to do is ditch the unneeded coin on the floor or somewhere.

Then you're set for the

grand
unveiling.

Basic Coin
Puzzle

Although there are hundreds of coin puzzles, this one qualifies as THE CLASSIC. Set ten coins up in a pyramid. Moving only **three** coins, change the pyramid so that it is pointing down instead of up.

...to this.

Don't read this if you don't want to cheat.

Solution: Shift 7 to the left of 2, 10 to the right of 3, and 1 below and between 8 and 9.

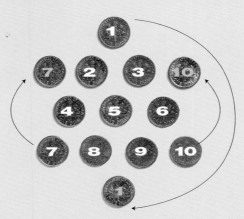

Caps and Quarters
Scam

A very, very special trick with a wonderful twist at the end. Great impact and yet another **Zero-**Practice Special. You'll need four or five bottle caps, plus a roll of clear tape.

What It Looks

Like: You ask to borrow a quarter from your very special friends. Explain that for hundreds of years, sidewalk charlatans have been cheating foolish tourists of their hard-earned money using a dirty little scam known as the pea-under-the-shell game. Explain that you'd like to do the same to them.

You borrow a quarter from your friends. Then you go into the kitchen (if you have to) to scrounge up a handful of identical bottle caps. You pass the bottle caps and the quarter around for inspection. Everything's normal. You give the quarter to one of your friends. Tell them to put it under one of the caps and start shifting the caps around. Concentrate carefully on the caps and tell your volunteer to stop after they've done some switching. Then you point to one of the caps. Sure enough, the coin's underneath it.

So they try it again. They switch the caps around even faster. And, just to make them even more frustrated, you don't pay much attention. You yawn. You act bored. You glance at your watch. When they stop, you point to the right cap instantly.

Your audience is gnashing their teeth. They're dying to fool you.

Your slimedog audience

Trick continues on the next page.

So you make it easy for them. For the Grand Finale, you offer to turn around **for the whole thing**. Tell your audience to move the quarter to a place under a different cap if they want and swap around to their heart's content. **You won't even watch!** When they're done, you turn around and get mysterious. You groan. You rub your temples. You're concentrating very hard.

Why are you concentrating so hard? Because most audiences are slimedogs. When your back was turned, they just kept the quarter. It isn't under ANY of the caps. They can hardly contain themselves they're so clever.

So. How do you deal with this? Simple. You bet your life savings that it's under the cap you're pointing at. Naturally, your audience is only too willing to take the bet. So you lift the cap. Big disappointment. Nothing there. Bye-bye life savings.
But are you worried?

No. You double the stakes. Twice your life savings. Naturally, your audience will be falling all over themselves to take the bet.

Then—the Big Moment: Point to the cap you've already lifted. The one that had nothing underneath it. ("I don't think I looked hard enough.")

42

Ask your audience to lift it up. Don't even touch it yourself. When they do, the quarter will be there. Just imagine their faces.

How to Do It?

It's a **slimy** little trick. (You're not sur- prised, are you?) Tape a single strand of hair to a quarter. Use a little piece of clear tape, (don't use the removable kind—it's too

In reality the tape and hair will be invisible.

frosty) and a piece of hair between 1 and 2 inches long. If you use clear tape, and lightish hair, people can hold the quarter in their hand, turn it over and inspect it, and they will never see the tape or hair.

Amazing but true.

Then using another piece of clear tape, stick another quarter inside a bottle cap.

You now have one gimmicked quarter, and one gimmicked bottle cap. You are ready to be amazing. Put the gimmicked bottle cap on the floor discreetly. Pass around the ordinary bottle caps for inspection. Once that's over, tell your audience to hide the quarter under one of the caps, and tell them to switch and swap the caps around, just like a sidewalk shyster.

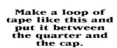

Make a loop of tape like this and put it between the quarter and the cap.

Trick continues on the next page.

43

Naturally, since there's a hair coming out from one of the caps, **it won't be hard to identify the cap** with the quarter underneath it, no matter how fast they move them.

Get them to move the caps around again. But get a little cockier with the second round. Look around. Inspect your fingernails. Your frustrated audience will switch and swap the caps around with lightning speed for minutes. When they're done, glance at the caps and pick up the guilty one. Laugh while they gnash their teeth. Toss the cap into the air for effect and when it drops to the floor because you missed it (you clumsy oaf) pick up the gimmicked one and make the switch.

For the Final Round. Turn your back on the whole thing. Your audience, like all audiences, will immediately hide the quarter so as to make you look like a fool. But since the gimmicked cap is now on the table, you're all ready for them. When you turn around, notice which cap is the gimmicked one (memorize something about its appearance). Go through all your acting, then lift it up. Nobody home. But when you set it down, do it hard. The coin will pop off the tape, and you'll be ready, a moment later, for the grand finale. Ask your audience to lift up the cap and...**lo and behold, the quarter is there!**

Which Hand?

A nice piece of small fraud that has a unique advantage: It works even if you botch it.

What It Looks Like

You're standing with a group of your worldly, **sophisticated** friends.

You reach into your pocket, pull out a handful of change and say something like, "OK, folks, it's Big Stakes Guessing Time. If you can tell me which hand this penny ends up in, I will provide you with a bona fide title and deed to the Brooklyn Bridge." You proceed to remove a penny from the handful, put the rest back in your pocket, and then...

IT'S SHOWTIME!

Trick continues on the next page.

You press the penny onto the back of your empty hand and push it hard with a couple of fingers. **Groan. Grunt.** Push harder until the coin has physically penetrated the hand entirely. Explain what you've done: **"Observe.** I have pushed this coin directly through the flesh of my hand."

Then, with both hands in fists, hold them out and ask the ageless question: **"Which hand?"**

No matter which hand they pick, they'll be wrong. And they'll be wrong for the next 45 times in a row if they think it was just luck.

How To Do It?

The magic here (as I have said so tediously before) is all in the show. The basic move is bald fraud. Right at the very beginning you didn't just take **one** coin from your handful (like you lied and said you did). You took **two.** Show one off, keep the other in a Finger Palm.

- ->

1 Keep one penny hidden in a Finger Palm. That puts one penny in each hand–one showing, one hidden.

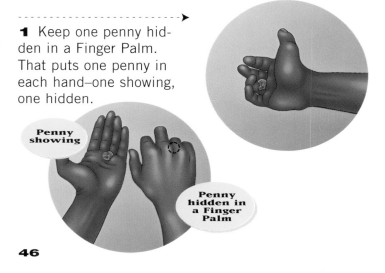

Penny showing

Penny hidden in a Finger Palm

2 Take the showing coin and place it on the back of your other hand, the one hiding a coin. Cover the showing coin with a couple of fingers and proceed to force it through the skin and bone of your hand (or at least **tell** them that's what you're doing...)

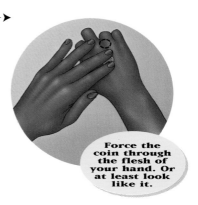

Force the coin through the flesh of your hand. Or at least look like it.

3 When you've finished that **incredibly** painful process, keep the coin covered and slide it back into your unoccupied hand.

If they pick this hand, open the other.

Ditto.

4 No matter which hand they point to, all you have to do is open the OTHER hand to reveal a penny.

("Sorry. Care to try again?")

The Best Coin
Trick
You've
Ever Seen

This is our favorite coin trick in the entire known universe. We have never seen another trick which combines a more amazing effect with less practice. **Period.**

What It Looks Like.

You set before your audience a clear drinking glass which is covered with a thin sheet of latex.* On top of the rubber sits a quarter. The glass is clearly empty. At your request, a volunteer steps up and pushes on the quarter with a fingertip. As she pushes, the quarter suddenly spits through the latex sheet and rattles around inside the glass. The effect is electrifying and totally unbelievable.

You can pass everything around for inspection. The latex sheet has no holes in it. The glass is completely normal, so is the quarter. And the most incredible thing is this: You never touched the quarter. Your volunteer did the whole thing.

*Stuck on inside back cover

Trick continues on the next page.

How to Do It:

There's no sleight of hand required. It's all in the preparation which, for discretion's sake, you should do in another room.

- ➤

1 Round up a small cylinder—the cap to a big marker, a lipstick tube, something like that. It has to be smaller around than a quarter and a couple of inches tall.

◀ -

2 Place a quarter on top of the cylinder as shown. Now get out the latex sheet which is stuck to the inside back cover.

Hold it as shown. Your task? Stretch the middle of it so tight that it becomes see-through clear. Pull in all four directions (north, south, east, west). You have to stretch pretty hard.

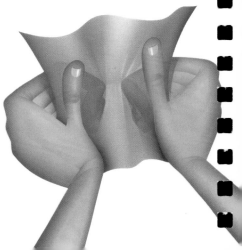

3 Press it over the quarter carefully...

seen from above

side view

...and pull it down below the rim of the quarter. Don't let go until the latex is tucked well under the quarter. If you do it right, you can release the latex, and the quarter will stay trapped in the latex. The hardest part of all this is keeping the quarter on its pedestal while you're pushing on it and trapping it in the latex.

Push straight down, keep a steady hand and just keep trying. You'll get it after a couple of tries. If you've done it right, the latex will be so tight over the quarter that it will be invisible (the latex, not the coin).

Trick continues on the next page.

4 Quarter is trapped in latex and *looks* like it's on this side...

...when it's actually on this side.

5 Set the latex with quarter on the glass. Secure with a rubber band.

The visual effect is stunning: The quarter looks as if it's on top of the latex, but it's actually on the underside.

From here on in, **it's showtime**. Take it to your audience. Don't let anyone else touch it (it's too special) but you can invite plenty of looking (it stands up to a very close inspection).

Then, step aside, bring in a volunteer and ask them to press on the quarter. It usually takes some fairly serious pushing, but when the quarter goes, it pops through so fast it's **freaky**. Now comes the moral test. Your audience will be stunned. But when they recover, they will be after your secret with ferocious intensity.

But remember: You are under oath!

You must NOT repeat this trick. Just smile, shrug your shoulders, and use your magic words...

"Did you like that? Well, let me show you something a little different then..."

*A note of warning: You'll only get about five or six usages out of the latex sheet before it tears, so don't waste this trick on your two-year-old sister. If you fall in love with this trick and have to have more sheets, you can order them from our catalogue. (See the back of the book for details).

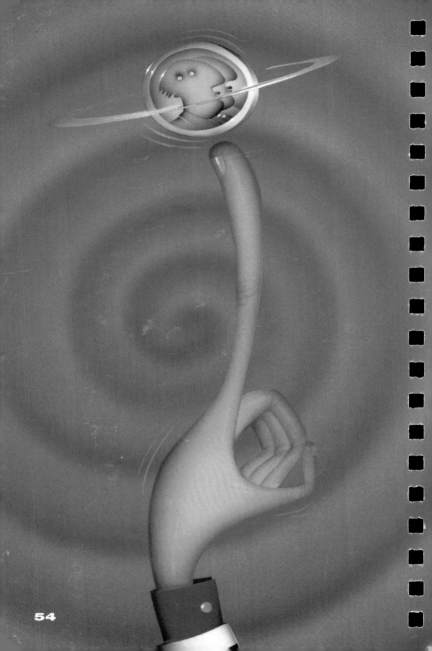

The Two-Headed Quarter Trick

Here's how it looks:

You pull a quarter from your pocket and ask your audience to gather around for a closer look. You explain what you're holding:

"Everyone has a hobby. I have a hobby making my own money in a little foundry I have in my basement. It's fun, it's creative, plus, I love what it does for me. Anyway, last night, something went wrong and a quarter came out with two heads on it."

As you're explaining, you're turning the coin over in your hands, revealing it to be, yes, entirely double-headed. **"But that's not all,"** you go on. **"It's weirder than that. If you whack it hard enough, you can knock it inside out. Then it's double-tailed."**

So you whack it once against someone's forehead, and sure enough, now it's double-tailed. Whack it again, and back it goes to double-headed.

"Weird, isn't it?"

Trick continues on the next page.

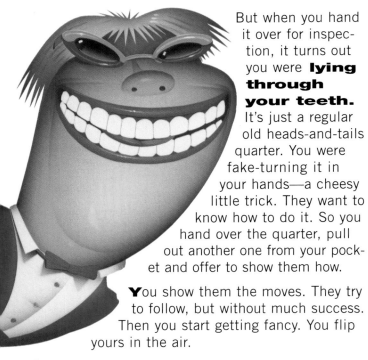

But when you hand it over for inspection, it turns out you were **lying through your teeth.** It's just a regular old heads-and-tails quarter. You were fake-turning it in your hands—a cheesy little trick. They want to know how to do it. So you hand over the quarter, pull out another one from your pocket and offer to show them how.

You show them the moves. They try to follow, but without much success. Then you start getting fancy. You flip yours in the air.

("Just make sure it flips an EVEN number of times. I count the flips in the air...")

You toss it back and forth. You turn it over again and again: It's ALWAYS heads. They keep trying to match you with their own quarter. But for them, the success rate isn't nearly the same. All you can do is shrug your shoulders. **"I guess it just takes practice..."**

How to Do It

You need to learn one simple move—the fake turn.

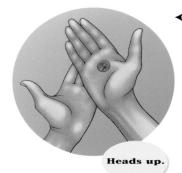

Heads up.

1 Put a quarter in your hand as shown, heads up. Then slap it down on the palm of your other hand, turning it over. This is a natural move, you've done it a million times, but this time...

2...concentrate.
Remember what your moving hands looked like.

Tails up.

3 Reveal.

Trick continues on the next page.

57

Here's how to practice it:

1 Put the quarter in your hand as shown. We'll make it easier by placing it near the edge of your hand.

Heads up.

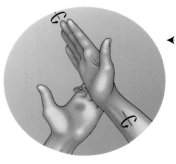

2 Then **just let it fall** by quickly pulling your hand out from underneath it. Since you didn't flip the quarter, you only pulled the "rug" out from underneath it, the quarter only falls, it doesn't flip. See the art for the motion. It's a very quick move that takes a bit of practice. (Think of your hand as a trap door and the quarter is sitting on top.)

3 Slap! Cover the coin. It's heads up under this hand.

4 See? Still heads up.

Heads up.

From here on in, it's nothing but practice.

You don't need to place the coin near the edge of your hand when you get good. You can set it down right in the center of your palm. And your "pulling out the rug" motion can look EXACTLY like the turning motion if you just work at it a little bit. After you've gotten the fake turn down, the rest of the trick is all theatre.

Put your real double-headed quarter in your pocket and begin everything with a normal quarter. Fake turn it back and forth. Hand it over with an offer to demonstrate the moves, pulling out the double-headed quarter for yourself. Since they're practicing with a **real** quarter, and you're demonstrating with a **double-headed quarter**, the possibilities are endless.

Have fun.

Credits

Acknowledgments:
Martin Gardner
Jay Alexander
Jeff Busby
Al Cohen

Needless Delays:
John Cassidy

Art Direction:
MaryEllen Podgorski

Design and Production:
Sandra McHenry Design

Illustration:
Bill Mayer
John and Judy Waller

Sourcing and Manufacturing:
DeWitt Durham

More Great Books from Klutz

The Buck Book

The Best Card Games in the Galaxy

The Official Icky Poo Book

Juggling for the Complete Klutz

The Klutz Book of Magic

Magnetic Magic

Peg Solitaire

The Puzzle Arcade

Kids Shenanigans

The Klutz Yo-Yo Book

The Klutz Catalog!

We hope you enjoyed reading **Coin Magic** as much as we enjoyed writing it! If you'd like to get **The Klutz Catalog,** just answer the **lengthy** questionnaire on the next page. Grab the nearest pen, fill in the blanks, tear it out, throw on some postage, and send it our way. Check out every dang thing we do (and activities too) on our website: **www.klutz.com**